Christmas Riddles

For Teens, Adults and Kids
#Stumped Volume 7

Copyright

ISBN: 9798724373722
Christmas Riddles - #Stumped Volume 7

INDEPENDENTLY PUBLISHED
PART OF THE STUMPED BOOK SERIES
STUMPEDRIDDLES.COM
ADMIN@STUMPEDRIDDLES.COM
TORONTO, ONTARIO, CANADA

Merry Christmas

Dedicated to Your
Loved Ones
for the
Holiday Season

TABLE OF *contents*

Table of Contents Continued Next Page

TABLE OF *contents*

Table of Contents Continued Next Page

TABLE OF *contents*

End of Table of Contents

"Turn the World off with a Smile"

Riddle Games

Word Play Party Games

Riddle games are ideal for family gatherings, dinner parties, baby showers, wedding showers, birthday parties, grad parties, and more. The best and worst riddle guessers get a prize or bragging rights, you choose.

Game 1

- Use a Timer
- Decide upon the amount of time to allow
- Read the Riddle
- Everyone shouts out answers
- The first one to guess the answer gets the point

Game 2

- Read the Riddle (with or without a timer)
- Everyone writes down their answer
- Put the answers in the middle
- Each person who guesses correctly gets a point

If nobody correctly guesses a riddle, everyone subtracts a point and goes backward on their total.

NOTE: Some of the riddles feature background photos. The photos are very subtle, indirect clues related to the riddle answer.

Chapter One
Santa Claus

Here you'll find riddle
answers that relate
to Santa Claus

Riddle 1

I'm a place to learn
and collaborate
I relate to toys, dads,
mechanical and wood,
I'm a busy place
creating surprises
especially for children
who are good?
What am I?

RIDDLE 2

THESE TWO WORDS SOUND THE SAME, BUT HAVE VERY DIFFERENT MEANINGS, SPELLED ONE WAY SAYS YOU'VE NAILED IT, SPELLED ANOTHER WAY, IT INVOLVES A 'BIT,' AND MAKES A ROMANTIC OUTING THAT'S SURE TO BE A HIT, WHAT TWO WORDS FIT ALL OF THIS?

Riddle 3

I apply to
fishing,
south,
vault,
north,
flag,
and fence
What word am I
that makes
sense?

Riddle 4

In one way this word
is unfeeling and unfriendly,
In another way
it has it's own song,
It's both a character
and a characteristic,
and that song is a
popular sing-a-long?
What word is it?

Riddle 5

I go with snow,
I go with space,
I go with jump,
and I go with case,
I fit with track,
I'm when things match,
I go with tie,
What word am I?

Riddle 6

Add an "s" and they can follow them, your, and our, On their own they range from evil to fun, but when it's Christmas, they're the good ones who get things done, Who are they?

Riddle 7

You know our names,
especially that famous one,
we play games when
we want to have fun,
children love us
on Christmas Eve,

Easy Alert !

Who are we that
they love to feed?

Riddle 8
Easy Alert!

Bleed,
Ring,
Dive,
Job,
and Brown,
What four-letter
word sits above
a smile or frown?

Riddle 9

I can be long or short,
white, brown, or black,
I'm on humans and goats,
but most known for
the one carrying the sack,
 What am I?

Riddle 10

I'm
a button,
a dance,
a laugh,
an ache,
and the most
recognized
Santa Claus trait,
What am I?

Chapter Two
Christmas Trees

These riddle answers are related to anything about Christmas Trees

Riddle 11

I'm something you take,
and used for displays,
you haul me out
on Christmas Day,
I apply to both
up and down,
and the positions
you're for,
What word am I
that you generally
do on a floor?

Riddle 12

I go
on a bed,
on a body,
and a tree,
I'm when you
avoid an issue,
and I can be mini,
What five-letter
word can I be?

Riddle 13

I'm the best marks
when you've aced
that test,
I can also spin,
am achieved when you win,
some call me a dog,
and I'm part of a tree,
Where are you when
you're standing on me?

Riddle 14

I'm part of a door,
and I can be dumb,
I'm even a bar,
and a church has one,
I pair up with whistles
when something has it all,
What word am I
that's even used to call?

Riddle 15

I'm a type of flood,
 and part of lime,
I'm the heads and tails
you see at night time,
during the holiday season
I flash and shine
if you see a white one
it might be your time,
What am I?

Riddle 16

Intelligence,
hearts,
grass,
and nails,
I am the
fill-in
when the
real thing fails,
What word am I?

Riddle 17

I sit up top,
and I can fly,
I'm also a cake,
and innocent eyes,
I'm a popular fish,
and famous falls,
and part of a team
that uses balls,
What am I?

Riddle 18

I'm a Judy,
I come with or
without light,
I can even have flowers,
or be green and bright,
what traditional holiday
decoration is part of
most celebrations?

Riddle 19

I'm an exchange,
an idea,
a basket,
and a shop,
what typical
holiday word
is even a box?

Riddle 20

A writing topic,
flowers,
bushes,
and a tree,
they all have
something in
common,
What can it be?

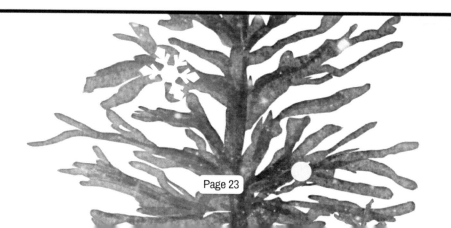

Chapter Three
Holiday Lights

The riddle answers are words
that relate to anything about
lights and lighting

Riddle 21

Said this way,
I've guided your way,
speaking each letter
I'm energy efficient
and better,
what double-meaning word
brightened the show
and also took you
where you wanted to go?

Riddle 22

I'm a theory, ham, quartet, and cheese, what word precedes or follows each of these?

Riddle 23

When the mind is this
the future is too,
vivid eyes are this
no matter their hue,
stars are this when
the sky is not blue,
What word am I?
Do I apply to you?

Riddle 24

These eggs can't
be scrambled,
this golf game
has no tee,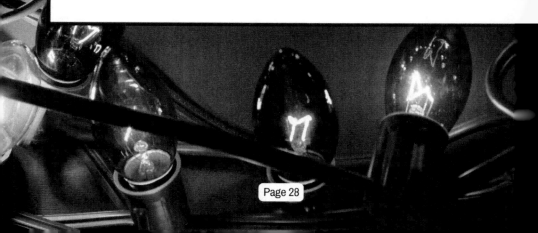
It's this above the knee,
and is a version of me,
What can this be?

Riddle 25

Choose the ones that are colorful or just go with basic white, put them in the ground, because in more ways than one, they're bright, you'll find them very useful, particularly at night, What are they?

Riddle 26

I'm attraction
and power,
I can create sparks,
and start fires,
I'm physical chemistry
and I run along wires,
What am I?

Riddle 27

Ear,
drain,
hair,
spark,
in,
and play,
all connect
to me in
some way,
What word am I?

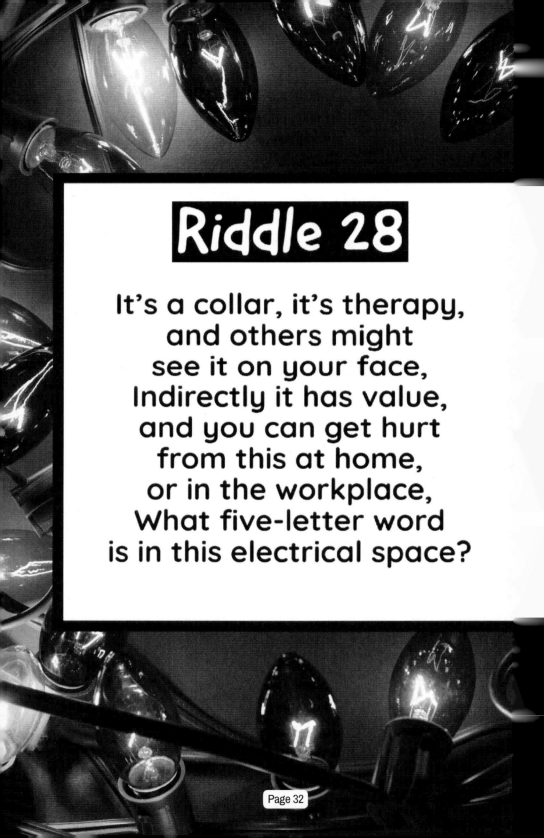

Riddle 28

It's a collar, it's therapy,
and others might
see it on your face,
Indirectly it has value,
and you can get hurt
from this at home,
or in the workplace,
What five-letter word
is in this electrical space?

Riddle 29

I'm an involuntary action,
but I can also be deliberate,
I'm cheesy when flirting,
and can refresh and prevent
a body part from hurting,
What action am I
that can be fast or slow,
and when held back
can mean shock or no!

Riddle 30

You might have
this about you,
it can happen
in the morning
or in the dark,
it can be worms
or a stick,
what four-letter word
applies to all of this?

Chapter Four
Winter Season

These riddle answers are
related to anything about winter

Riddle 31

I make things white,
I block your sight,
I'm always cold,
I can't be controlled,
I'm always severe,
and something to fear,
stay in today,
and out of harms way,
What am I?

Riddle 32

I'm
a bite,
a warning,
and a jack,
it doesn't get
any easier than that!
What am I?

Easy Alert !

Riddle 33

I'm a type of slope,
and I can be sneaky,
I'm a challenging road,
and hands made
for cheating,
I'm also a fish,
and a floor
after cleaning,
What am I?

Riddle 34

I'M A WAY TO STIPULATE ESCALATION, BUT ALSO SOMETHING YOU THROW, KIDS ESPECIALLY LOVE THESE, AND IN BOTH SITUATIONS I CAN GROW, WHAT AM I?

Riddle 35

Food in your mouth, buckets of bull, clearing a path, or preparing holes, what are you doing when these are your goals?

Riddle 36

I'm when you eat quickly,
and something you wear,
I'm made of many materials,
and can cover your hair,
I can be cheap or expensive,
come plain or with flair,
What am I?

Riddle 37

YELLOW ME CAN STING,
OR YOU CAN WEAR ME
IN WINTER OR SPRING,
I KEEP YOU WARM
OR I CAN SWARM,
WHAT SIX LETTER
WORD AM I?

Riddle 38

IN TECH TERMS
I CAN BE WHITE OR BLACK,
IN BOOK TERMS
I'M THAT FAMOUS CAT,
IN THE WINTER MONTHS
I'M IN A KID'S BACKPACK,
OR SOMETIMES YOU'LL
FIND ME ON A RACK,
WHAT THREE-LETTER WORD AM I?

Riddle 39

I'M SOMETHING YOU CAN BE IN PHYSICALLY OR MENTALLY, I'M ALSO A DOOR, A SCREEN AND A TROOPER, AND THE ONE THING THAT YOU DON'T WANT TO BE SUPER, WHAT AM I?

Riddle 40

I'M A FUND RESERVED FOR RAINY DAYS, AND A MELTED MESS DURING SPRING'S EARLY DAYS, I PROVIDE EXTRA SECURITY WHEN YOU HAVE TO PAY, BUT AM NOT FAVORED FOR OUTSIDE PLAY, WHAT AM I?

Chapter Five
Holiday Foods

These riddles are food items
relating to the Christmas
holiday season

Riddle 41

I'M A MILK PUNCH
AND A SEASONAL FAVORITE,
ADD BOOZE TO ME
OR DRINK ME STRAIGHT UP,
BUY ME OR MAKE ME,
HAVE ME COLD,
OR HEAT ME UP,
WHAT AM I?

Riddle 42

WHEN YOU'RE ECCENTRIC, **CRAZY,** AND FILLED WITH CANDY, AND NUTS, WHAT ARE YOU?

Riddle 43

Your pillows,
your face,
envelopes,
peppers,
and chicken,
all have this
eight-letter word
in common,
What word is it?

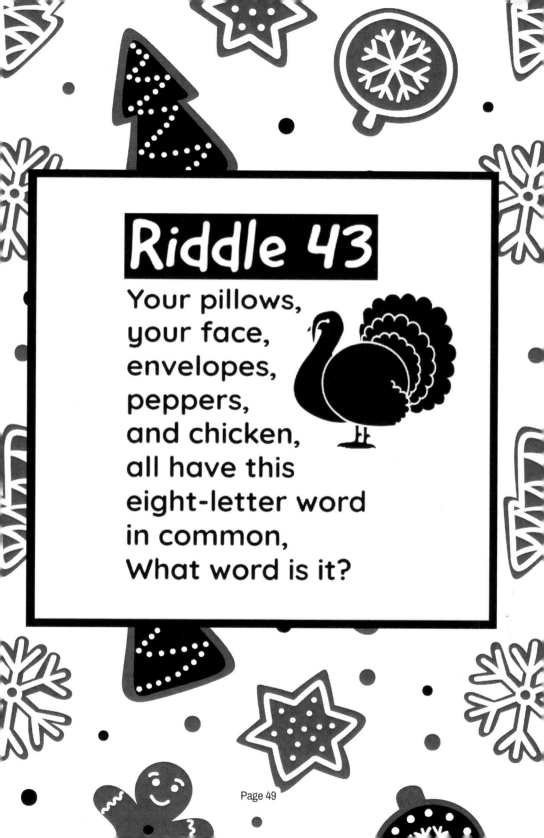

Riddle 44

I can be a neck,
a country,
a vulture,
a burger,
and your dinner,
What am I?

Riddle 45

I'M A HOUSE, AND A MAN, DECORATE ME IF YOU CAN, FOR SELFISH REASONS THE FOX IS MY BIGGEST FAN, WHAT AM I?

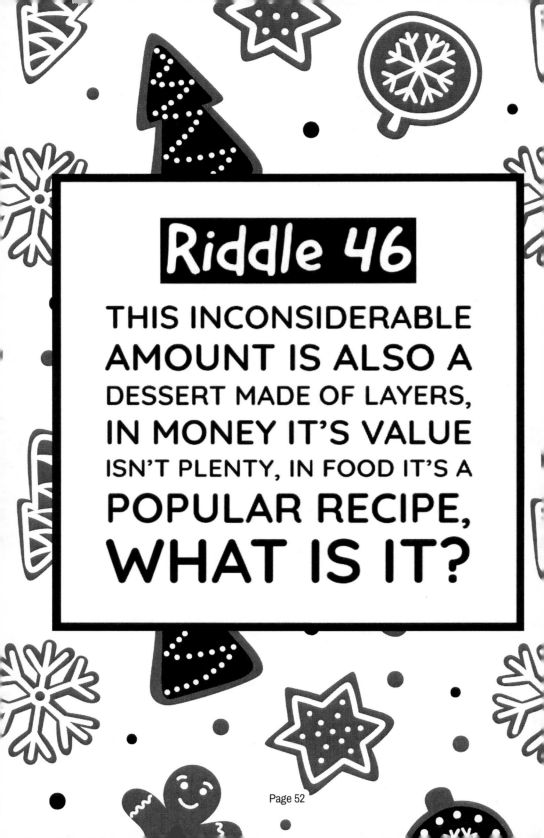

Riddle 46

THIS INCONSIDERABLE AMOUNT IS ALSO A DESSERT MADE OF LAYERS, IN MONEY IT'S VALUE ISN'T PLENTY, IN FOOD IT'S A POPULAR RECIPE, WHAT IS IT?

Riddle 47

I'M BLOOD,
CUPS,
RICE,
BREAD,
CHOCOLATE,
POPS,
AND VANILLA,
WHAT AM I?

Riddle 48

IT'S A BURGUNDY JUICE AND SOMETIMES DRIED, TO IMPROVE YOUR HEALTH THE VITAMIN VERSION IS TRIED, AS MUFFINS OR SAUCE YOU MIGHT EAT THEM 'TIL YOU DROP

WHAT IS IT?

Riddle 49

I'M A SHOWOFF,
OR A HOG,
I GO WITH
EGGS AND CHEESE,
WHAT THREE LETTER
WORD WORKS WITH
ALL OF THESE?

Riddle 50

MOST EVERYONE LOVES IT, IT'S HARD TO RESIST, IT CAN BE VERY RICH AND LAND ON YOUR HIPS, FROM MILK TO MOUSSE WHAT NINE-LETTER WORD IS THIS?

Chapter Six
Festive Things
These riddles are items or
things that are festive
for the holidays

Riddle 51

I HELP CIRCULATION, CAN EASE PAIN, AND EVEN HELP VARICOSE VEINS, STRANGELY ENOUGH I'M A CHRISTMAS FAVE, WHAT AM I?

Riddle 52

WHEN YOU CELEBRATE, REVEL, AND PRAY, AND RAISE YOUR ARMS AND SWAY, WHAT ARE YOU DOING?

Riddle 53

I'M THE WHEEL OF THE YEAR,
AND REPRESENT ETERNAL LIFE,
I CAN BE A CROWN,
AND AM ALWAYS RING–LIKE,
CREATE AND DECORATE ME,
OR I'M SOMETHING YOU CAN BUY,
WHAT PRETTY GREETING AM I?

Riddle 54

WE GO DOOR TO DOOR,
WE SELL YOU NOTHING,
WE ASK FOR NOTHING,
WE COST YOU NOTHING,
WE LOVE TO SHARE JOY,
WE'RE ADULTS, GIRLS, AND BOYS,

WHO ARE WE?

Riddle 55

I'm the redeemed outcast,

I'm Valentino,

I'm a song,

I'm a book,

and TV show,

What am I?

This one is easy,

you must know?

Riddle 56

What word does
typewriter,
dance,
candy,
and presents
have in common?

Riddle 57

I'M A BIRTHDAY,
A MESSAGE,
SEASONS,
VIRTUAL,
AND A CARD,
WHAT EIGHT-LETTER
WORD AM I?

Riddle 58

Do this for

Mom,

Your life,

Our differences,

and the good times,

What 9 letter word am I?

Riddle 59

I'M HOT,
I'M BEAUTIFUL,
I'M ELECTRIC,
I'M GAS,
WHAT NINE LETTER WORD AM I,
QUICK, GUESS ME FAST!

Riddle 60

Light,
Heat,
Holders,
and scents,
I'm famous
in the wind,
What's the word
that makes sense?

Chapter Seven
Family Time

These riddles are things to do with the family at Christmas Time

Riddle 61

YOU CAN DO THIS TO
A HOME,
A CAKE,
A TABLE,
A TREE,
A WALL,
AND COOKIES
WHAT IS IT?

Riddle 62

WHETHER REINDEER, OR ONLINE, THIS FIVE LETTER WORD IS ABOUT FUN, ESPECIALLY WHEN YOU'VE WON, WHAT'S THE WORD?

Riddle 63

I'M A KEEPER,
I'M LOCAL,
AM PART OF WORK,
AND ONLINE,
I CAN COST YOU MONEY
FROM FOOD TO WINE,
WHAT FOUR-LETTER
WORD AM I?

Riddle 64

I can be a
network,
a drawing,
a character,
and a show,
What seven-letter
word am I?
Do you know?

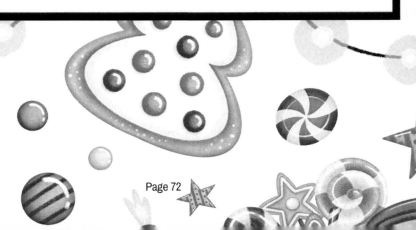

Riddle 65

This five-letter word
can be part of a
festivity or celebration,
It's what you do with your
eyes when you dwell
with gratification,
What is the word?

RIDDLE 66

ALONG,
A SONG,
AND DANCE,
CROON,
REJOICE
AND CHANT,
WHAT WORD
AM I?

Riddle 67

I am
supplies,
an animal,
a rental,
a girl,
dresses,
and time,
what five-letter
word am i?

Riddle 68

This six-letter word
is something you do
around,
together,
and up,
What is it?

Riddle 69

This five-letter word
is part of mine,
a trade,
a witch,
a table,
and beer,
it's also a hobby that
might have a lot of gear,
What word is it?

Riddle 70

HAND ME DOWN, I'M PART OF YOUR FAMILY, I'M YOUR BELIEFS, AND DEFINE YOUR RAISING AND REALITY, WHAT WORD AM I THAT IS UNIQUE TO VARIOUS PARTS OF HUMANITY?

Chapter Eight
The Meaning of Christmas

These riddles are related to things about the meaning of Christmas

Riddle 71

I'm a day,
a plan,
a weight,
and a certificate,
What word am I?

Riddle 72

THIS SIX-LETTER WORD
IS A PLACE TO SLEEP,
WHERE HORSES CAN EAT,
AND AT CHRISTMAS TIME
IS CONSIDERED
HUMBLE AND SWEET,
WHAT WORD IS IT?

Riddle 73

I'M A FAMOUS DIAMOND,
AND WHAT WE ALL SHOULD HAVE,
WITH ME IN YOUR HEART
DIFFICULT TIMES AREN'T SO BAD,
I'M PART OF A FAMOUS SONG
ABOUT LIFE'S DANCE,
AND I GIVE YOU STRENGTH
TO TAKE THAT CHANCE,
WHAT FOUR-LETTER WORD AM I?

Riddle 74

I'M THAT FAMOUS SCENE DISPLAYED DURING THIS TIME OF YEAR, THE STARS OF THE SEASON ALL GATHERED HERE, I REPRESENT THE BIRTHDAY BOY'S HOLY PREMIER, WHAT EIGHT-LETTER WORD AM I?

Riddle 75

I'm a celebrated arrival
four weeks before,
I'm also a calendar
with multiple doors,
chocolate or trinkets
relate to me,
what six-letter word
can this possibly be?

Riddle 76

I'm a celebration,
a large lump or shape,
at this popular gathering
the outfit includes a cape,
production is also
possible this way,
but for this riddle book
it's a place you can pray,
What is it?

Riddle 77

He delivered a message
to Jesus' Mom,
that she would carry
the blessed one,
Do you know your angels?
he carried a lily,
Can you name this messenger?
This one is easy!

Riddle 78

Bells,
a building,
and weddings,
apply to me,
you usually visit
to set your soul free,
or just to 'be',
This one is easy!
What am I?

Riddle 79

I'm a meanie,
miser,
grump
and hater,
answer quickly!
it's easy,
Who am I?

Riddle 80

I'M A FIRST,
AND A GIVEN NAME,
I'M UNIVERSALLY KNOWN
AS CHRISTMAS TIME
IN ANOTHER LANGUAGE,
WHAT WORD AM I?

Answer
Section

Chapter One Answers
Santa Claus Riddles

1. Workshop

2. Sleigh/Slay

3. Pole

4. Frosty

5. Suit

6. Elves

7. Reindeer

8. Nose

9. Beard

10. Belly

Chapter Two Answers
Christmas Tree Riddles

11. Stand

12. Skirt

13. Top

14. Bells

15. Lights

16. Artificial

17. Angel

18. Garland

19. Gift

20. Evergreen

Chapter Three Answers
Holiday Lights Riddles

21. LED/Led

22. String

23. Bright

24. Mini

25. Bulbs

26. Electricity

27. Plug

28. Shock

29. Blink

30. Glow

Chapter Four Answers
Winter Season Riddles

31. Blizzard

32. Frost

33. Slippery

34. Snowball

35. Shoveling

36. Scarf

37. Jacket

38. Hat

39. Storm

40. Slush

Chapter Five Answers
Holiday Food Riddles

41. Eggnog

42. Fruitcake

43. Stuffing

44. Turkey

45. Gingerbread

46. Trifle

47. Pudding

48. Cranberry

49. Ham

50. Chocolate

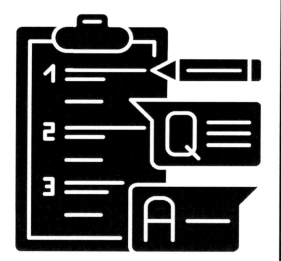

Chapter Six Answers
Festive Things Riddles

51. Stockings

52. Rejoicing

53. Wreath

54. Carolers

55. Rudolph

56. Ribbon

57. Greeting

58. Celebrate

59. Fireplace

60. Candle

Chapter Seven Answers
Family Time Riddles

61. Decorate

62. Games

63. Shop

64. Cartoon

65. Feast

66. Sing

67. Party

68. Gather

69. Craft

70. Tradition

Chapter Eight Answers
The Meaning of Christmas Riddles

71. Birth

72. Manger

73. Hope

74. Nativity

75. Advent

76. Mass

77. Gabriel

78. Church

79. Scrooge

80. Noel

Back Cover Answer

Eve

Write Your Own Riddle

Here's your riddle challenge. Try to write your own riddle. You'll start with the answer, then go from there.

The answer is:

"Cookies"

Write your completed riddle in the box. Good Luck!

HI, I'M BARBARA.

I'm here to help you take your mind off this crazy life for a little while. Take a break from your demands and wrap your mind around solving riddles.

Whether for fun, a game, a personal challenge, a distraction, or brain exercise, these riddles are meant for you and that break you need.

For as long as I've known, I've been able to write riddles, one-liners, quotes, sayings, and poems. To put this quirkiness to use, I put together a series of riddle books featuring original riddles in the 'what-am-I' format.

ABOUT

SOCIAL MEDIA

INSTAGRAM

Instagram.com/riddlechallenge

FOLLOW

FACEBOOK

Facebook.com/stumpedriddles

THE WEBSITE

Stumpedriddles.com

Get Your Free Downloadable Book

SELF CARE WORD SCRAMBLE
For Teens and Adults

Subscribe
www.stumpedriddles.com

TIKTOK

tiktok.com/@stumpedriddles

...and Twitter.com/stumpedriddles

MORE STUMPED ACTIVITY BOOK FUN

Simple Game Books or Personal Challenge - Stumpedriddles.com

STUMPED SUDOKU BOOKS

STUMPED WORD SEARCH BOOKS & MORE

STUMPED RIDDLE BOOK SERIES

 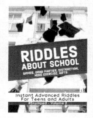 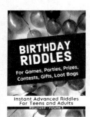 

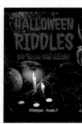   

FREE DOWNLOAD

stumpedriddles.com/free-downloadable-book/

Made in United States
Cleveland, OH
28 November 2024

10982820R10065